Paul T. Semms

The 10 Millionaire Commandments

How to become a millionaire? How to get rich?

10 simple rules.

The 10 Millionaire Commandments
Copyright © 2014 / 2016

All rights reserved by the author. No part of this publication may be reproduced, stored in a retrieval system, or transmitted in any form or by any means, electronic, mechanical, photocopying, recording, or otherwise, without the prior permission of the copyright owner. All other rights including printing, movie, audio book, video game adaptation or translation are also with the author and copyright owner.

Pictures

Cover:
businessman and drawing chart © *peshkova - Fotolia.com*

Other Pictures:
frau kein geld © *Peter Atkins - Fotolia.com*
Golden Growth © *mipan - Fotolia.com*
Time is money concept © *Sashkin - Fotolia.com*
glück © *frank peters - Fotolia.com*
Glücksbringer Kleeblatt © *Aamon - Fotolia.com*

Tables and Figures: Paul T. Semms

ISBN-13: 978-1540389923

ISBN-10: 1540389928

How to become a millionaire?

For most people „being a millionaire" is an unrealistic dream. But this goal is easier to accomplish than you think.

In this guide you'll find 10 simple rules that can help you getting rich and maybe at one point in time a real millionaire.

Complex, endless books with thousands of detailed tips have no sustainable effect. You buy them, read a little and never transform these ideas into real actions. Therefore, this guide focuses on short and simple rules that are food for thought. Always keep these simple rules in mind and continuously improve on your way to become a millionaire.

Getting rich is not easy and there is of course no guarantee for success. You need to take action. You need a plan and you have to implement it.

Lots of success !

1.

Save money, save money, save money!

As we all know, the chances of winning the lottery are extremely low. So you need to start saving money to be able to achieve your dream of getting rich.

The earlier in life you start with this, the better is your chance to save millions. Therefore start today by maximizing your monthly savings rate. There is no time like the present. The sooner you lay money aside, the faster your capital grows through the compounded interest effect (see rule no. 6).

Analyze your monthly income and expenses accurately and calculate the amount that you can save each month. Of course, this sum should be as high as possible.

How can you increase your monthly saving rate?

1) Increase your revenues (e.g. plan and make a career, achieve a higher salary, start a second job, create a business, …).

If you have found the right partner (e.g. wife or husband) don't forget to provide strong support to enable your partner to grow and to develop her/his career and income. Two salaries are always better than just one.

2) Optimize or reduce your expenses.

Focus your spending on things that are important for you. Always ask yourself if the piece you want to buy really makes you happy. Do not waste your money! E.g. you can optimize your insurance or food (it should be healthy!) costs. If you buy an apartment or a house you will save rental costs (but only if the monthly payment is not much higher than your current rent).

"Take care of the pence and the pounds will take care of themselves."

E.g. if you manage to increase your savings per month by only 200$, it already adds up to 2.400$ per year or 24.000$ in 10 years … and this even without compounded interest.

Best practice is to transfer these monthly savings to a separate bank account always at the beginning of the month. Why on the beginning of the month? If it is already gone, you don't get used to it.

2.

Don't live beyond your means.

Only spend as much as you have! Only invest in things that will save or make money long term.

Don't live beyond your means! Be aware of your financial circumstances. Remember your monthly savings rate and learn how to optimize it. Never purchase e.g. a car or other household objects on credit. These objects don't last forever, they lose value every minute and with using a credit you will pay for years and months – not a good investment. An you will pay interest … and at the end you will pay too much! Don't forget that someone earns money with giving you a credit.

Summarized: don't finance daily-life goods, cars or similar things with credits. Only use credits to finance e.g. property for own use or into property as an investment. In objects that will last and where you are sure that you will get an acceptable price if you sell them. If you live e.g. in your own flat, this will avoid paying rent and at the end can save you money. As an exercise take a deeper look at your statements of accounts for the last months and calculate your monthly income and expenses. In addition don't forget the annual costs (costs that incur only once a year) convert them on a monthly basis. An example:

Income (net cash) per month	
Wife	3.000
Husband	4.000
Sum (net cash per month)	**7.000**

Expenses per month:	
Home Loan Financing	800,00
Insurance 1	150,00
Insurance 2	120,00
Church donations	50,00
Other Donations	28,00
Phone/Internet	55,00
Electricity, Water, Heating	150,00
Garbage Collection	8,00
Cable TV	30,00
Gas (for the cars)	300,00
Eating at work	200,00
Food	500,00
Clothes	300,00
Gifts	50,00
Sum (Expenses per month)	**2.741,00**
plus annual costs converted to monthly basis	214,17
TOTAL	**2.955,17**
Max. monthly saving rate	**4.044,83**

Expenses per Year (Annual Costs):	
Fitness-Club	75,00
Insurance House	1.000,00
Insurance 3	80,00
Insurance 4	100,00
Insurance 5	55,00
Car 1	133,00
Car 1	400,00
Car 2	300,00
Membership Car Association	79,00
House Costs 1	48,00
Other Taxes	300,00
Sum of all annual costs:	**2.570,00**
Annual costs converted to monthly costs (/12):	**214,17**

The maximum monthly savings rate would be 4044 Dollars in this example. This sum can be further optimized.

© Peter Atkins - Fotolia.com

3.

Make a Plan.

Make yourself an ambitious financial plan and look at the beginning of each month, how much you've saved and how large your current assets are.

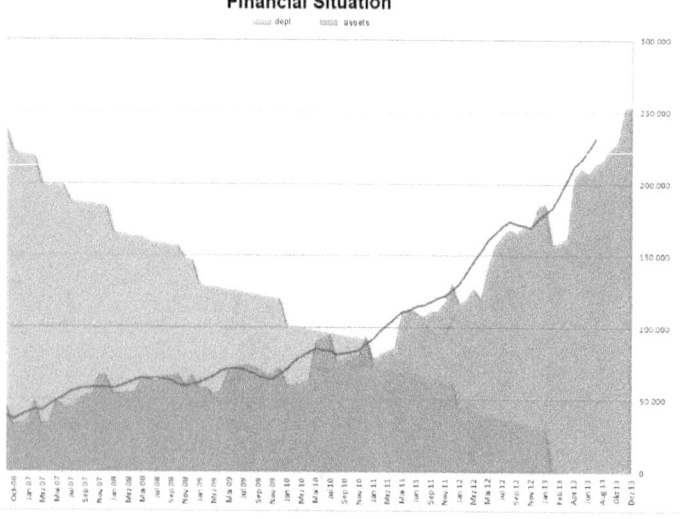

A plan helps you to clearly define your goals and enables you to check on a regular basis if you adhere to it. If your assets are developing faster than initially planned that's great – but then adapt the plan by increasing your savings estimate. If you are behind, start thinking what you can change, how you can further increase your savings rate. How can you reduce your expenses? How can you increase your income?

It is extremely satisfying and motivating to see in writing what you have already achieved.

© mipan - Fotolia.com

4.

Envy doesn't help.

Envy isn't a helpful or useful feeling. It only makes you feel inadequate. So get rid of it. If anyone is more successful than you, then ask yourself how he or she has achieved this success and learn from it, instead of feeling sorry for yourself.

You are in most cases the reason for failure. Don't look for a scapegoat. You have to work on yourself if you want to change something. Try harder, try it again, change something.

5.

Earn money!
Maximize your income.

How can you maximize your income? If you're self-employed, look for new and additional business opportunities. Think about how you can offer better and more profitable services or products? Can you attract more customers through optimized or targeted advertising? Are you at all in the right business? What are the next trends in the industry from which you can benefit?

If you're an employee, ask yourself how you can climb up the career ladder. Is this realistic or should you look for other revenue opportunities outside your current job? Why not working on new business ideas, starting your own business e.g. an internet business (see Rule 7).

6.

Let your assets work for you!

Your investments have to work for you, because this is the only way you can benefit from the compound interest effect.

In the following you find a brief example of this effect. Every year your investment grows because interest is paid. And in the following year you earn again interests on your grown investment (grown by last year's interest). This effect is quite impressive.

Average Interest Rate:	2%	4%	6%	8%
Initial Investment:	**100.000**	**100.000**	**100.000**	**100.000**
Year 1	102.000	104.000	106.000	108.000
Year 2	104.040	108.160	112.360	116.640
Year 3	106.121	112.486	119.102	125.971
Year 4	108.243	116.986	126.248	136.049
Year 5	110.408	121.665	133.823	146.933
Year 10	121.899	148.024	179.085	215.892
Year 20	148.595	219.112	320.714	466.096
Year 30	**181.136**	**324.340**	**574.349**	**1.006.266**

With an initial investment of 100.000$ and an average

interest rate of 4% you have more than 324.000$ after 30 years. At an interest rate of 8% you have more than 1.000.000$! Of course it will not be easy to get 8% on average, but remember that you will add each month your monthly savings rate to this amount.

At an average interest rate of 4% and a monthly savings rate of only 1.000$ (and 100,000$ initial investment) you will have saved almost a Million US-$ after 30 years. Play a little bit with the numbers and adjust them to your own circumstances. Over the years you might be able to increase the monthly savings rate or start even with a higher amount as in this example.

Important:
Start now with your personal savings plan! The more time the better for the compound interest effect!

Always invest your money wisely and without emotions. Don't take too much risk, don't put all eggs in one basket, the diversification of risk is key. Invest e.g. parts of your assets in stocks or investment funds, another part in short-term and long-term loans, parts in real estate, etc.

Only invest money in businesses, opportunities or funds you clearly understand. It makes no sense to put your money in high-risk technology stocks when you don't understand how the market or industry works or what the potential future of a technology is. But if you understand a market and your are convinced of a success e.g. of a new product, then you can take a certain risk. Closely monitor the performance of your investment and rather realize a loss if your investment/shares fall below a threshold (e.g. 20% lower than your purchase price) in order to prevent a total loss of your investment.

© Sashkin - Fotolia.com

Calculated Risk.
Failure can happen.

From time to time you can also take a calculated risk. But only use small parts of your savings for risky projects. This ensures that in case of a failure or complete loss of this investment you are not thrown back by years regarding your financial planning.

Allocate only a small percentage of your funds (max. 10-15%) for risk investments.

If you have a great business idea, give it a try...just do it. Focus first on ideas that require a minimum start-up investment e.g. a website or internet services that will lead to immediate earnings from the beginning. Be realistic, pragmatic and don't fool yourself: if you look at many business ideas more closely you will see that they can't work. The product, the location and the price must be right. If you fail with your idea take the positive side: you can learn a lot from failed ideas or projects. Next time you can use your new experience.

Most millionaires have not made their fortune with their

very first business idea. Some have even failed several times, but never gave up.

© frank peters - Fotolia.com

8.

Think positive!

Believe in your success! Only if you are convinced of your idea you can influence others and yourself with positive energy. Being optimistic increases automatically your own engagement, commitment and creativity. Going through life with a smile always helps.

© Aamon - Fotolia.com

9.

Being an entrepreneur?

Most millionaires are entrepreneurs. This does, of course, not mean that everyone starting his/her own business is getting rich. However, setting-up an own business with a great business idea will increase your chances to be successful.

If you are a little bit risk-averse, maybe try some smaller projects or ideas to test possible future independence and entrepreneurship in parallel to your regular employment if this is allowed (see Rule 7).

It also helps if your partner can support you or if you can use money from investors to work on your ideas.

10.

What do you expect from life?

To know yourself, your dreams, your wishes and what you expect from life is essential.

Ask yourself: what is really important to me?

Family, partnership, career, leisure, sports, friends, influence, power, wealth, ...?

Only if you know what you want you can get it. Be aware of your own needs and goals in life. Maybe "Being rich or being a millionaire" is no longer as important as you really thought.

Therefore take some time, take a look on the next two pages and write down your goals in life. Use this time to really actively and comprehensively think about what you really want. Unfortunately many people are often driven by the goals of others.

What do I really expect/want from life?

How much money/assets do I have today?

_____

How much money do I want to have in...

...10 years? _____

...20 years? _____

...30 years? _____

What are my business ideas?

_____

_____

_____

_____

_____

_____

_____

_____

_____

_____

...and always remember the ten commandments to get rich:

1. Save money, save money, save money!

2. Don't live beyond your means!

3. Make a plan!

4. Envy doesn't help.

5. Earn money. Maximize your income.

6. Let your assets work for you!

7. Calculated risk. Failure can happen!

8. Think positive!

9. Being an entrepreneur?

10. What do you expect from life?

Lots of success!

www.ingramcontent.com/pod-product-compliance
Lightning Source LLC
Chambersburg PA
CBHW070720210526
45170CB00021B/1388